Y0-ARM-655

I Do,
Now Let's
Eat!

I Do, Now Let's Eat!

A Cookbook for Newlyweds

By P. Michele Talley

Outskirts Press, Inc.
Denver, Colorado

The opinions expressed in this manuscript are solely the opinions of the author and do not represent the opinions or thoughts of the publisher. The author has represented and warranted full ownership and/or legal right to publish all the materials in this book.

I Do, Now Let's Eat!
A Cookbook for Newlyweds
All Rights Reserved.
Copyright © 2010 P Michele Talley
v2.0

This book may not be reproduced, transmitted, or stored in whole or in part by any means, including graphic, electronic, or mechanical without the express written consent of the publisher except in the case of brief quotations embodied in critical articles and reviews.

Outskirts Press, Inc.
http://www.outskirtspress.com

ISBN: 978-1-4327-4477-9

Outskirts Press and the "OP" logo are trademarks belonging to Outskirts Press, Inc.

PRINTED IN THE UNITED STATES OF AMERICA

Table of Contents

Congratulations

Compliments of:

_____

Wine Selection

- **Sauvignon Blanc** – *white or light fish, mild cheese, fruit*
- **Chardonnay** – *grilled chicken, salmon, shellfish, and grilled fish, anything with a cream sauce.*
- **Pinot Noir** – *light meats, chicken, grilled anything, salmon.*
- **Merlot** – *pasta, red meat, duck, smoked or grilled foods*
- **Zinfandel** – *tomato pasta dishes, pizza, pesto, red meats, chicken with heavy sauces*
- **Cabernet Sauvignon** – *red meats, especially a juicy barbequed steak, grilled and smoked foods.*
- **Syrah** – *red meats, spicy pizzas, herbed sauces on red meat, turkey*
- **Dry Rosé** - *salads, pasta salads, barbeque chicken or fish, light spicy foods*
- **Moscato Castello del Poggio d` Asti** - *This is a wonderful wine that goes well with appetizers, entrees and desserts. I first had this wine at Olive Garden and it has become one of my favorite wines.*

Foreword From Nigel....

One of the most stressful moments for some newlyweds is not the honeymoon night, but rather the first day in the kitchen, when the honeymoon is a distant memory, and the realities of life begin to kick in.

Well no more! When I first learned that P. Michele Talley was writing a cookbook designed for newlyweds, I immediately appreciated what an ignored and important void she would fill. With so few cookbooks geared toward the inexperienced couple, writing this book made perfect sense. Her casual, non-intimidating approach puts the novice cook at ease, and the anecdotes from other couples gives you that "if they can do it, we can do it too" motivation to try all the recipes.

In this day and age, we live in a world that is driven by our insane schedules and fueled by our need to succeed. We're constantly trying to squeeze more time out of that narrow window on our calendar that is already jam packed with business meetings, dentist appointments, dog grooming or whatever else keeps our agenda chock-full of deadlines.

"I Do, Now Let's Eat" will make you exhale, open the door to your newly 'married' address and say, 'Honey, I am home! Let's cook!'

You see, one thing I have realized during my years as a Chef and restaurateur, preparing meals with ingredient lists that read like a novel, is that the simplest meals always turn out the best, the tastiest, and gets you the most praise. There is also no better way to enjoy a meal than in the company of the ones you love most. Though this may seem cliché. I honestly feel that the smells, tastes and togetherness that appeal to the senses during these moments engrave lasting memories in our brains, which mere pictures can never recall.

When I was employed as a food stylist at the Food Network in New York City, I worked my way through my fair share of cookbooks. In our test kitchens we each had our favorite "die-hard" cookbook that we wouldn't part with. We would always joke and say that any cookbook without at least four great recipes wasn't worth printing.

I am way past that number in this book, and still counting.

So, enjoy this book together, create beautiful and tasty dishes that will make you and your partner go into fits of giggles every time you remember trying to figure out how to pronounce quiche (it's pronounced *ke-esh*) or what end of a spatula to use to fend off the vultures the first time you prepare Thanksgiving dinner. You guys made it this far; this book will only strengthen your relationship and your love. You will laugh, you will cry (it's in the onions), but you will love this book. The recipes are simple enough for the beginner, yet exciting and worldly enough to "wow" the in-laws. After all, they were assembled by a globe trekker who has ate her way around the world, and we are all lucky that she decided to share the best of her tasty memoirs in this book.

So, forget the stress for a moment and grab your other half, it's about to get messy and fun!

Chef Spence is the owner and Executive Chef of **Ripe Kitchen and Bar** in Mt. Vernon, NY. An alumnus of the esteemed **Culinary Institute of America**, Nigel is best known for his numerous appearances on a variety of shows including: *Food Network's* **Throwdown with Bobby Flay, Chopped, Everyday Living** on **Martha Stewart Radio,** the **Today Show with Kathie Lee and Hoda** (NBC), **Neighborhood Eats** (ABC), **Tony's Table** (CBS) and Air Jamaica's *Island Stylee*. **Ripe Kitchen and Bar** has also received critical acclaim from media giants such as the *New York Times, the Journal News, Westchester Magazine, Jamaica Eats, Skywritings* and the *Jamaican Magazine.*

A Word From Heather.....

After the wedding, many couples find the honeymoon glow can grow cold when it comes to standing in front of an empty refrigerator and trying to figure out what to feed two hungry mouths every night for dinner.

But instead of considering cooking as a chore, I recommend that couples use the opportunity to reconnect each evening over dinner, spending meaningful time discussing the days events – and this book is designed to help you do just that!

The kitchen will grow to be the heart of your home, so take these newlywed days to embrace the art of learning simple, special meals that you will both enjoy.

Inspired by her travels, Michele Talley, I Do, Now Let's Eat! offers you easy-to-prepare recipes along with clever tips and useful herb, spice and measurement guides.

And with recipes that call on authentic ingredients and fresh flavors from around the globe, consider it an extension of your honeymoon, after all – date night doesn't need to take place in a restaurant. Make a meal from a region of the world you'd like to visit together one day and spend some time planning all the places you'll go in your journey along the path to marital bliss!

From appetizers for easy entertaining to main course meals and some sweet desserts, you and your honey will devour every aspect of this how-to. Just keep in mind that the secret ingredient to any meal, just like any marriage is pure and simple, *Love*.

Heather Snively, Celebrity Wedding Planner. She has been seen on hit TV shows including **The Style Network's "Married Away"** and **"Who's**

Wedding Is It Anyway", *Platinum Weddings, E!, iVillage Live!, Inside Edition, The Learning Channel, The Daily Buzz, FOX News* and *Lifetime TV's "Get Married"*. Her regular contributions appear in the pages of *InStyle, People, Grace Ormonde, The Knot, Elegant Bride, Brides, Bridal Bride, Orlando Leisure,* and *Orlando Style* with a monthly column. Her point of view and tips on trends and all things wedding have been featured in *The New York Times, Wall Street Journal, Boston Globe, Orlando Sentinel, Orlando Business Journal* and *Copley News Service*. Find her expertise online as the ongoing Central Florida Expert at **The Knot.com**.

A Letter From

Great book! Beautiful cover! What more can I say? Let's eat! After owning a winery and dealing with brides, grooms, and their wonderful weddings for a few years, this is a refreshing addition to the wedding repertoire. Written by a wonderful lady with great taste and a flair for food. We can't cook and have that lovely, mellow evening every night, so savor these recipes and let them last. Try a few each week and enjoy the idea that who you are sharing it with makes what you are sharing that much more enjoyable.

I Do, Now Let's Eat! Is for everyone who loves to cook and loves to eat.

Don't we all? Thank you Michele.

Love each other, Peace
Mitchell Gordon, Author
"Love in the Verbal Garden", Part One

Down Memory Lane

My Mother was the second oldest daughter in a family of eight children and says she began cooking at age 7. I believe her because when I was growing up she was always in the kitchen cooking and baking. She made homemade candies and cookies and at an early age she introduced my siblings and me to classics like fondue, paella, stir-fry's and many other world cuisines. The neighborhood kids looked forward to the giant sub sandwiches piled high with different types of meats, cheeses and tons of vegetables and then drenched in Italian salad dressing. Subway couldn't touch my Mom when it came to subs. Being of mixed heritage Mom felt she was a citizen of the world and it was important to her to incorporate the foods from many countries into her daily cooking.

After I became an adult, I too continued to cook the recipes that she passed down to me as well as others that I gathered from family members, friends, co-workers and my years in the travel industry. As my daughter's began to cook they asked me how to make this and that and I began writing down recipes for them. They planted the seed for this cookbook. One day a couple was in my office for help with their honeymoon and I told them about the Beef Stroganoff story from so many years back and a light went off in my mind and the idea for a cook book for newlyweds was formed.

So this cookbook is years of many trials and errors, of disasters and of successes. Don't worry you can do this, start with the simplest recipes and build up to the recipes that require a little more time and energy. Experiment with the spices and make each recipe your own. Remember breakfast can be dinner sometimes.

Joy to you,
P. Michele

To my Daughter's,

Latica, Bianca and Ambra I am so blessed you are in my life. Thank you for your continued support and love. I thought about what I could say that would express my hope for you in this life. This is from your Mother with love. Always put your trust in Him and…

Live simply. Love generously. Care deeply. Speak kindly.
Leave the rest to JAH.

Acknowledgements

Christina, my thanks goes out to you for your creativeness and for understanding my ideas. Thank you to www.allrecipes.com for the images and to Sarita Lynne. A very special love shout to my sister Ori-Oma and Aunt Betty for being my cheerleaders. To Janice, Addie, Barbara, Gwen, Betty, Sarita Lynne, Gail and Patrice my friends and supporters, Bull's-eye! Life is beautiful. To my Boardies hat's off to you thanks for the stories, fun times and memories. To my play brother Danny you are American Dread. To family and friends too numerous to name, my love and thanks…

Love,
P. Michele

What's For Dinner?

A few months after I had been married I decided to cook Beef Stroganoff for my husband. I had been to a family gathering at my Aunt's house and she had made this dish and it was delicious. So I asked her for the recipe. In her recipe one of the main ingredients was stew beef so after a trip the grocery store I was ready to cook. I browned the stew beef and added all the ingredients just as I had written down. I boiled my noodles and tasted the sauce of the stroganoff and to my delight it tasted just like my Aunt's. I made a salad and some dessert and I set the table with the wedding gifts we had received and everything looked beautiful.

I have to tell you at this point in my young life I knew the basics of cooking. I could make great breakfast and sandwiches but I had a desire to stretch out and try different recipes. In comes my hubby all smiles and ready to eat. After he freshens up we sit down to eat or rather he will eat, as I am too nervous to think about eating. I watch my husband take a bite of the stroganoff and begin chewing and chewing and while he is doing this he is looking at me with this strange expression on his face. After about a minute he finally says to me as he discards the meat into a napkin "Baby, I can't eat this it's tough like rubber bands" seeing the expression on my face he adds " but the salad looks good". At that moment I wished the ground would have opened up and swallowed me. Later I told my Mom who told me stew beef is tough and has to be cooked a long time to tenderize it, a fact my aunt forgot to mention. It's funny now but at the time I was so embarrassed and at that very moment I was determined to learn how to really cook.

So Congratulations! My hope this cookbook will be the start of wonderful memories. It's true nothing says I love you better than a good home-cooked meal.

Enjoy!

Appetizers & Beverages

Chicken Chili

Best Little Meatballs

- I bag of frozen meatballs
- I jar grape jelly
- I bottle of Heinz chili sauce

In a large saucepan, empty bottle of chili sauce and jar of grape jelly. Heat over low until smooth. Add frozen meatballs and cover and simmer for 1 hour. Use toothpicks for serving.

Tip: You can transfer meatballs to a crock-pot to keep warm.

Chicken Chili

- 4 skinless chicken breast
- 2 cans red beans
- 2 cans white northern beans
- 1 12 oz jar of salsa
- ½ cup sugar
- 1 10 oz bag of Monterrey jack and Colby cheese mix
- Salt and Pepper

Season chicken breast with salt and pepper and place in an oiled baking dish and bake on 350 degrees for 30 to 35 minutes. Remove chicken breasts to a plate and allow to cool to the touch. Using 2 folks begin shredding the chicken. Place shredded chicken, red beans, white northern beans, salsa and sugar into a large pan and simmer for 30 minutes. Remove from heat and stir in cheddar cheese. Serve with tortilla chips.

Tip: *This dish tastes even better if you make it the day before and refrigerate and reheat the day of serving. This way the flavors have time to blend.*

Spicy Shrimp

- 12 Jumbo shrimp, peeled and deveined
- 2 Jalapeno peppers, seeds and ribs removed
- ½ cup fresh lemon juice
- 1 tablespoon cilantro, chopped
- 1 tablespoon parsley, chopped
- 2 garlic cloves
- ½ cup olive oil plus 2 tablespoons
- ½ teaspoon salt
- 1 lime, quartered

Combine peppers, lemon juice, cilantro, parsley and garlic in a blender and puree until smooth. While blender is running add ½ cup of olive oil and blend until well combined.

In a bowl add shrimp and blended marinade and toss fully covering the shrimp. Refrigerate for 20 minutes. Heat 2 tablespoons of olive oil in a large sauté pan over medium heat. Add shrimp and cook for 2 minutes on each side until shrimp turn opaque. Transfer to a plate and sprinkle with salt and squeeze lime quartered over the shrimp. This goes great with Mango Margaritas. Serves 3 or 4.

Mango Margaritas

- 4 ripe mangos
- I can frozen limeade
- I ½ cups of margarita mix reserve ¼ cup
- ¼ cup sugar
- 3 ounces tequila
- 4 cups crushed ice
- Course sugar for dipping
- Lime slices

Peel and slice mangos and combine with limeade, margarita mix, sugar and tequila in a blender for 15 seconds. Add crushed ice and blend until margaritas are slushy. Rub edge of margarita glass with lime and dip into reserved ¼ cup of margarita mix and course sugar. Pour margaritas into glasses. Serves 6

Tip: Chill margarita glasses in freezer several hours before serving

Tropical Fruit and Dip

30 years ago - oh my! On our honeymoon, we drove to Florida, we returned in the middle of the night from driving, we were starving, tired, etc., everything was closed - did I mention we were hungry? Anyways, when we got into our apartment, opened the fridge, it was fully stocked. My Mom was a Godsend; she had gone in and stocked our fridge full - what a great and pleasant surprise!!!! I absolutely loved her for doing that. That is a just a wonderful thing to do for a newlywed and a wonderful "wedding" present.

- 2 (8 oz.) package fruit flavored cream cheese
- I small container Cool Whip
- 2 (7 oz.) jars marshmallow cream

Cream the cream cheese. Add marshmallow cream and blend well; add Cool Whip. Serve with chunks of pineapple, strawberries, cantaloupe, bananas, mango slices, apples, grapes and papaya slices.

Orange Julius

- 1 (6 oz.) can frozen concentrate orange juice
- 1 cup milk
- 1 cup water
- ½ cup sugar
- 1 teaspoon vanilla extract
- 6 glasses of ice cubes

Place all ingredients except ice in a blender and blend for 30 seconds. Pour over ice. Serves 6.

Jerk Chicken Drummettes

In Jamaica, the Jerk Men normally come out in the evenings. I always get this late at night with a slice of bread and ketchup. Yummy!

- 1 or 2 pounds chicken drummettes
- 1 scotch bonnet pepper (jalapenos may be used)
- 2 tablespoon thyme
- 2 tablespoon allspice
- 4 cloves garlic
- 2 medium onion
- 2 tablespoon sugar
- 2 tablespoon salt
- 2 tablespoon black pepper
- 2 tablespoon ground cinnamon
- 2 tablespoon nutmeg
- 2 tablespoon ginger
- ½ cup olive oil
- ½ cup soy sauce
- Juice of one lime
- ½ cup orange juice
- ½ cup white vinegar

Place all ingredients except chicken into a food processor or blender to make a jerk sauce. Wash and clean chicken drummettes. Pat dry. In a large freezer bag add chicken and the jerk sauce reserving some of the sauce for dipping. Shake to mix and place chicken in refrigerator to marinade overnight. On a hot grill slowly cook chicken until done basking with remaining marinade while cooking. Serves 6 to 8.

Tip: For best results add a rack of pimento wood to barbeque grill. Normally this dish is made with a whole cut up chicken. I like the little drummettes when entertaining guests. You can make this using pork instead of chicken too.

Lemon Mint Spritzer

- I quart ginger ale
- I cup chilled grape juice
- ½ cup lemon juice
- ½ cup sugar
- 5 or 6 mint leaves
- 2 cups ice water
- Lemon slices
- Ice cubes

Combine ginger ale, grape juice, lemon juice, water, and sugar in a large pitcher and mix well adding more sugar to taste if necessary. Stir until sugar dissolves. Chop mint leaves and add to the pitcher. Serve in glasses with ice cubes and garnish with lemon slices. Serves 6.

Fried Green Tomatoes

- 4 large, firm green tomatoes, sliced
- I cup all-purpose flour
- I cup cornmeal
- Salt
- 2 teaspoons black pepper
- Vegetable oil for frying

Slice tomatoes to desired thickness. Place sliced tomatoes out on a pan and sprinkle with salt. Transfer and drain tomato slices in a colander and allow time for salt to pull the water out of the tomatoes approximately 45 minutes. Mix flour, cornmeal and pepper. Coat tomatoes in mixture and deep fry until golden brown on each side.

Tex-Mex Pizza

- 1 package of taco seasoning
- 2 cans refried beans
- 2 cups sour cream
- 3 large tomatoes, chopped
- 1 large onion, chopped
- 2 small cans black olives, chopped
- 2 cup shredded cheese (any kind you like)

Mix taco seasoning with sour cream. Layer on a pizza pan in the following order: Refried beans, sour cream mix, tomatoes, onions, olives and cheese. Chill and serve with nacho chips.

Wake up Baby Spritzer

- Juice from 3 oranges
- Juice from 2 lemons
- 1 cup pineapple juice
- 1 cup water
- 1 quart ginger ale
- ½ cup sugar
- 2 teaspoons grenadine
- Ice cubes
- Lemon and orange slices

Combine orange juice, lemon juice, pineapple juice, water, ginger ale, sugar and grenadine in a large pitcher. Add more sugar to taste if necessary. Blend well until sugar dissolves. Add lemon and orange slices to pitcher and pour into glasses filled with ice cubes. Garnish glasses with a slice of lemon.

Authentic Cuban Mojitos

- I lime
- I teaspoon powdered sugar
- 2 ounces white rum
- 2 ounces club soda
- I sprig of mint
- Crushed ice

Put mint leaves into a Collins glass and squeeze the lime juice over them. Add the powdered sugar and muddle (crush) the mint, lime juice and sugar together. Add crushed ice. Stir in the rum and top off with club soda. Garnish with mint sprig.

Sugared Peanuts

- 2 cups raw shelled peanuts, skins on
- I cup sugar
- ½ cup water
- ¼ teaspoon salt

Preheat oven to 300 degrees. In a saucepan over medium heat, dissolve sugar and salt in water. Add peanuts. Stir frequently, until peanuts are completely coated and no syrup left in saucepan. Spread the peanut mixture onto ungreased cookie sheet separating the peanuts as much as possible. Bake for 30 minutes, stirring every 5 minutes. Remove from oven and let cool. Makes 2 cups.

Tip: *Try this with several types of raw nuts. It's great!*

Relish Tray

- 12 celery sticks
- 12 green onions, tips removed
- 12 radishes
- 1 cup black olives
- 1 cup green olives
- 12 dill pickles
- 12 sweet pickles
- 12 carrot sticks
- Cauliflower and broccoli broken into bite size pieces

Wash and drain vegetables and arrange in groups on a relish tray or on a serving plate. Refrigerate and serve cold. Serve with your favorite dip.

Champagne Sparkler

- 2 bottles Champagne
- 4 wine coolers (12 oz each)

Combine champagne and wine coolers and pour into carafes and chill. Chill wine glasses in freezer several hours before serving. Serves 6.

Deviled Eggs

- 1 doz. eggs, boiled
- ½ cup salad dressing
- ½ cup sweet pickle relish
- 2 tablespoons mustard
- 1 tablespoon sugar
- 1 tablespoon salt
- 1 tablespoon pepper
- Paprika for garnish

Peel boiled eggs and cut lengthwise in half. Scoop out yoke a put in a medium boil. Place egg white halves on a plate. Using folk break up yoke. In a small bowl add mayonnaise, pickle relish, mustard, sugar, salt and pepper. Mix well. Add mixture to egg yokes and mix well. Use a spoon or pastry bag and fill each egg white half with mixture. Sprinkle each egg with paprika. Serves 6.

Mint Iced Tea

- 4 cups water
- 2 tablespoons sugar
- 2 tablespoons honey
- 5 teaspoons green tea leaves
- 6 mint sprigs
- 1 three inch piece ginger peeled and sliced
- 1 lemon, cut in quarters

Combine water, sugar, honey, mint sprigs and ginger in a large saucepan and bring to boil. Reduce heat and simmer for 5 minutes. Add the green tea and simmer for another 5 minutes. Strain and let cool. Serve over ice and garnish with lemon. Serves 4.

Chili Con Queso Dip

- 1 pound ground beef
- 1 can Rotel or 1 cup of your favorite Salsa
- 2 pounds Velveeta cheese

In a large skillet brown ground beef and drain off oil. In a large saucepan over low heat melt cheese, stirring frequently. When cheese is melted add can of Rotel tomatoes or Salsa and stir. Add the ground beef and mix thoroughly. Serve with Tortilla chips.

Tip: You can melt the cheese in the microwave. Stir frequently.

Soups
& Salads

Rotini Rainbow Salad

Pineapple Cashew Salad

- ½ cup sweet white wine, Riesling or ice wine
- 1 ½ cup of pineapple, peeled, cored and diced
- ¼ cup packed brown sugar
- ½ cup roasted cashews
- 4 mint leaves, finely shredded

In a medium bowl pour wine. Add sugar stirring until dissolved. Add pineapple cubes. Cover and refrigerate 2 hours. When ready to serve stir cashews into the pineapple. Divide and sprinkle with mint and serve. Serves 6.

Mixed Salad with Feta Cheese

- 1 head Bib lettuce
- 1 bunch watercress
- 1 cup golden raisins
- ½ teaspoon balsamic vinegar
- 3 tablespoons fresh lemon juice
- 1 teaspoon minced garlic
- 2 tablespoon extra-virgin olive oil
- Salt and pepper to taste
- 1 cup feta cheese

Wash watercress. Discard old lettuce leaves, then wash. Wrap greens in paper towels and refrigerate. In a small saucepan put raisins and cover with water and cover and simmer for 3 minutes. Remove saucepan from heat and set aside allowing raisins to plump. In large salad bowl combine oil, lemon juice, vinegar, garlic and salt and pepper. Mix well. Just before servicing remove greens from refrigerator and tear into large pieces. Drain raisins. Add greens and raisins to marinade mixture and toss well. Sprinkle with feta cheese on top. Serves 4.

Gazpacho

- 1 cucumber, halved and seeded but not peeled
- 2 red bell peppers, seeded and peeled
- 4 plum tomatoes
- 1 red onion
- 3 garlic cloves, minced
- 3 cups tomato juice
- ¼ cup olive oil
- ¼ cup white wine vinegar
- ½ tablespoon kosher salt
- 1 teaspoon fresh ground black pepper

Roughly chop the cucumbers, tomatoes, red onions and bell peppers into 1 inch cubes. Put each vegetable separately into a food processor and pulse until coarsely chopped. Do not over process!

After vegetables are processed, combine them in a large bowl and add garlic, tomato juice, vinegar, olive oil, salt and pepper. Mix well and chill. The longer the gazpacho chills the more flavors it will develop.

Avocado and Grape Tomato Salad

When we got our first place together we were very poor and thought love was going to get us through everything...lol... We moved into an attic loft with an awful décor, one solitary couch and an annex kitchen which contained a tabletop stove with 2 burners. No worries we had hardly any money but we figured we could survive on tinned food until better times came along. So, off we went and bought the makings of a meal from cans.... We got back to the flat, stored it away and smugly thought we had done quite well. Yep, we were going to have a feast on our first night away from our parent's homes. We were all grown up now, in our own flat. Yeah?? NOT! We forgot to buy a tin/can opener. We dined on white bread and cheese and onion crisp. Accompanying condiment: mint sauce out of a jar...

- 1 ½ cups of Grape Tomatoes, quartered vertically
- 1 ripe avocado, diced
- ¼ cup red onion, diced
- 1 garlic clove, diced
- 3 tablespoons cilantro, chopped
- 1 small jalapeno pepper, seeded and diced
- 1 tablespoon honey
- Juice of 1 lime
- ¼ teaspoon ground cumin
-

Gently combine all ingredients in a medium bowl. Add salt to taste.

Tip: This can be eaten with tortilla chips or place on top of grilled fish or chicken

Peach Salad with Warm Bacon Vinaigrette

- 1 (5 ounce) bag baby spinach
- 2 peaches, peeled and sliced
- 1 pint fresh raspberries
- 1 cup toasted almonds
- Goat cheese garnish (optional)

Wash spinach and wrap in paper towels. In a large bowl, combine dry spinach, raspberries, almonds, and peaches. Drizzle with warm bacon vinaigrette. Toss gently to coat. Garnish with goat cheese.

Warm Bacon Vinaigrette

- 2 tablespoons butter
- 2 tablespoons light brown sugar
- ¼ teaspoon salt
- 2 teaspoons cornstarch
- 2 teaspoons shallot, chopped
- 2 tablespoons water
- ¼ cup raspberry balsamic vinegar
- 4 slices bacon, cooked and crumbled

In a small non-stick saucepan, melt butter over medium heat, add shallot and cook for 2 or 3 minutes. Remove from heat set aside. In a medium bowl, whisk together brown sugar, salt and cornstarch. Slowly whisk in water and vinegar. Add crumbled bacon and vinegar mixture to saucepan with shallows and cook over medium heat. Stir constantly for 4 minutes until mixture thickens. Serve immediately. Serves 4.

Mom's Rotini Salad

- 12 ounces rotini, rainbow
- 2 medium tomatoes, chopped
- 1 small green pepper, chopped
- 1 small onion, chopped
- 1 small cucumber, chopped
- 1 cup fresh broccoli, flowerets
- 1 cup fresh mushrooms, sliced
- 8 ounces Italian salad dressing, bottled
- 1 cup black olives, pitted & sliced
- 8 ounces pepperoni slices

Bring 4 quarts of water to a rapid boil and cook Rotini according to package. Drain. Rinse in cold water. Combine with remaining ingredients. Cover and chill. Toss salad before serving. Serves 6 to 8.

Taco Salad

- 2 lbs. Ground beef
- ½ head lettuce
- 1 medium onion
- 2 medium tomatoes
- 1 package taco seasoning
- 1 can red beans
- 1 can tomato sauce
- 1 cup shredded Colby cheese
- ½ cup black olives, chopped
- ½ cup green olives, chopped

Brown ground beef in skillet, drain. Chop onions, tomatoes, and olives and place in large bowl. Add red beans, tomato sauce, shredded cheese, ground beef and taco seasoning to tomato and olive mixture. Add lettuce last so it won't become soggy. Mix well. Serve with Doritos or your favorite corn chips. Serves 6.

Summer Corn Salad

- 4 ears fresh corn
- 1 pint of grape or cherry tomatoes
- 1/3 cup red onion, diced
- ½ cup basil leaves, chopped
- ¼ cup parsley, chopped
- 4 ounces of feta cheese, crumbled
- ¼ cup olive oil
- 2 tablespoons red wine vinegar
- Salt and Pepper to taste
- 4 cups water

In a large pot bring water to a boil over high heat. Peel husk off corn and place corn in pot of water and boil for 7 to 10 minutes or until tender. Cool slightly. Cut kernels off corn and put in a medium bowl. Add remaining ingredients and toss. Season to taste with salt and pepper.

Tortilla Soup

I first had this in Puerto Vallarta Mexico and it was so delicious I came home and practiced how to make this recipe. It's a great comfort food on a chilly night.

- 3 Tbs. Olive oil
- I onion, chopped
- 3 ears of fresh corn or I can (15 oz.) whole kernel corn, drained
- I can (15 oz.) of tomato sauce
- 2 tbs. Cumin
- 3 cups of vegetable broth
- I tbs chipotle chili chopped
- 2 cups of Colby cheese cut into cubes
- 3 avocados peeled and chopped
- ½ cup of fresh cilantro chopped
- 8 corn tortillas cut into ¼ inch wide strips

Heat oil over medium heat in a large skillet and cook onions until transparent about 5 minutes. Cut corn off cobs and add to onions in the skillet and cook until lightly browned.

Transfer onions and corn into a large dutch oven or cooking pot. Add tomato sauce, broth, cumin, chipotle chili, avocado, cheese and cilantro. Stir. Simmer over low heat for 30 minutes. Add corn tortillas last. Continue simmering for several minutes and serve in soup bowls. Serves 6.

Tip: *Soup should be made the day of serving to get the right consistency to avoid sogginess.*

Southern Potato Salad

- 6 potatoes, peeled, boiled and cubed
- 1 ½ cup salad dressing
- ¾ cup sweet pickle cubes
- 2 tablespoons yellow mustard
- 1 onion, finely chopped
- 2 eggs, boiled and sliced
- 8 ounce sour cream
- 2 tablespoons sugar
- Salt and pepper to taste
- Paprika for garnish

In a large bowl add cooled potato cubes and remaining ingredients. Mix thoroughly, but do not over mix. Sprinkle with paprika and garnish with egg slices. Serves 8 to 10.

Fresh Cucumber and Tomato Salad

- 1/2 cup extra virgin olive oil
- 2 tablespoons balsamic vinegar
- 2 tablespoons red wine vinegar
- 1/2 teaspoon sea or kosher salt
- 3 small fresh cucumbers
- 2 large beefsteak tomatoes, vine ripened

Peel cucumbers and slice tomatoes into wedges. Place tomatoes and cucumbers in salad bowl and sprinkle with sea salt or kosher salt.

Combine olive oil with vinegars, whisking together well. Drizzle over tomatoes and cucumbers; serve at room temperature.

Potato and Leek Soup

- 3 Leeks
- 4 Potatoes, quartered
- ¼ cup butter
- ½ cup milk
- ½ cup light cream
- 1 quart water or chicken stock
- ½ teaspoon fresh chopped parsley
- 2 tablespoons chopped celery
- 2 tablespoons shallots
- Croutons (optional)
- Salt and pepper to taste

Peel and quarter the potatoes.

Prepare the leeks by removing the green portions. Cut down the center lengthwise and wash thoroughly. Chop the white portions finely and sauté lightly with the chopped shallots in half the butter for 5-7 minutes. In a large pot add the water or chicken stock, celery, potatoes, and simmer 20-25 minutes. Remove potatoes and leeks to a small bowl, mash to a puree and return the puree to the pot. Stir in the milk, cream, and remaining butter, reheating one minute if needed. Season to taste with salt and pepper. Garnish with parsley and croutons. Serves 4

Greek Salad

- 1 green pepper, sliced in rings
- 1 red onion, finely sliced
- 1 medium cucumber, sliced
- 3 medium tomatoes, cut in thin wedges
- 2 ounces Kalamata olives, pitted
- 6 or 7 ounces slice of feta cheese
- 1/2 fresh lemon or juice
- extra virgin olive oil
- fresh oregano or thyme leaves
- salt and pepper

In a large flat salad dish, or plate combine sliced vegetables with olives and tomato wedges. Lay slice of feta on top and drizzle with olive oil, squeeze lemon over that and sprinkle with oregano or thyme and salt and pepper. Feta can be cubed or crumbled.

Apple Pear Salad

- 2 apples, sliced
- 2 pears, sliced
- I stalk celery, sliced
- 2 tablespoons fresh orange juice
- I teaspoon grated orange rind
- I tablespoon honey
- ¼ tablespoon salt
- ¼ tablespoon ground cinnamon
- ¼ tablespoon ground nutmeg
- Salad greens

Mix apple, pear and celery slices. Mix orange juice, honey, salt, cinnamon and nutmeg in a medium bowl. Pour over apple mixture; toss until evenly coated. Cover and refrigerate at least 1 hour. Arrange apple mixture on salad greens

Angel Hair Pasta with Broccoli and Shrimp

- 8 large shrimp, peeled
- 3 large garlic cloves
- 1/2 teaspoon salt and pepper
- 6 tablespoons olive oil
- 6 tablespoons butter
- 1 bunch of broccoli, cut up
- 8 oz. angel hair

In a mixing bowl with lid toss together Shrimp, garlic, salt and pepper and 4 tablespoons olive oil. Cover. Marinate the shrimp for 3 hours in the refrigerator. After marinating, remove the garlic pieces. Heat 2 tablespoon of olive oil and 3 tablespoons butter in a saucepan and sauté shrimp for 2 or 3 minutes, until pink.

In a large saucepan, add broccoli and bring to a boil cook 3 minutes and drain and return to saucepan; cover. Cook pasta according to directions. Drain.

Toss everything together. Serves 2.

Easy Chicken Soup

- 2 packets dry chicken noodle soup mix
- ½ gallon of water
- 1¼ pound of left over cooked chicken, diced
- small onion, diced
- 1 medium potato, diced
- 4 sticks celery, diced
- 1 large carrot, diced
- salt and pepper, to taste
- 1 tablespoon vegetable oil

Heat oil in a large soup pot and stir fry onion. Do not brown. Add other vegetables and chicken and stir-fry for a few minutes.

Cover with water and add chicken noodle soup mix. Simmer for 30 minutes. Serves 6 to 8.

Layered Green Peas Salad

- 1 (10 ounce) package thawed green peas
- 1/4 cup chopped onion
- 1/4 cup sliced celery
- 1/4 teaspoon salt
- 1/8 teaspoon pepper
- 1/8 teaspoon dried basil
- 1/3 cup sour cream
- 1 teaspoon sugar
- 3/4 cup shredded Cheddar cheese
- 6 slices bacon, cooked and crumbled

Layer first 9 ingredients in order given in a 1 quart serving bowl. Cover and chill at least 4 hours, top with bacon, and toss salad just before serving. Serves 4

Corn and Cheese Chowder

- 2 cups of cream style corn
- ½ cup water
- 2 cups potatoes, diced
- I cup carrots, sliced
- I cup celery, celery
- 2 tablespoons chopped onion
- I teaspoon dill
- I ½ cup milk
- 2/3 cup of grated cheese
- Salt and pepper to taste

In a large stockpot add all ingredients. On medium heat stir frequently. Do not boil. Serve with cornbread. Serves 4.

Rum Soaked Tropical Fruit Salad

- 2 Mangos, peeled and cubed
- 2 bananas, peeled and sliced round
- 2 oranges, peeled and sectioned
- 1 cup fresh pineapple, chunks
- 1 star fruit, sliced
- ¼ cup light rum
- ½ cup coconut, toasted and grated

In a glass bowl mix all fruit except coconut. Pour rum over fruit and mix well. Refrigerate for 30 minutes. Sprinkle coconut over mixture and serve immediately. Serves 4 to 6.

Tuna Macaroni Salad

- I cup of macaroni shells
- 6 ½ ounce can tuna, drained
- ¼ cup pickle relish
- 1/3 cup salad dressing
- I teaspoon yellow mustard
- 2 eggs, boiled and chopped
- I tablespoon lemon juice
- 2 tablespoons sugar
- Salt and pepper to taste

Cook macaroni shells according to directions. Drain thoroughly. In large bowl, break up tuna. Add cooked shells and pickle relish. In another bowl, blend salad dressing, lemon juice, eggs and salt and pepper. Mix all ingredients thoroughly. Serves 4.

Entrees

Michele's Husband Proof
Beef Stroganoff

Asian Baked Chicken

- 1 Cut-up whole Chicken
- 1 tablespoon of vegetable oil
- ½ cup of water
- 1/3 cup of Soy sauce
- 1/3 cup of brown sugar
- 1 tablespoon of Ketchup
- ¼ cup of Apple juice
- ¼ tablespoon of crushed red pepper
- 2 garlic cloves-minced
- 1 green onion-chopped

Place chicken in a large plastic bag. Mix together remaining ingredients and pour over chicken. Seal bag and place in a bowl in the refrigerator or for several hours. Arrange chicken in a large shallow baking dish with the marinade. Bake at 350 degrees for one hour basting once or twice. This chicken is delicious hot or cold.

Lemon Crusted Baked Tilapia

- 2 lbs. Tilapia fillets
- ¼ cup olive oil
- ¼ cup lemon juice
- 2 tablespoon salt
- 2 tablespoon lemon-pepper seasoning
- ½ cup seasoned bread crumbs

Preheat oven to 350 degrees. Place fillets in a shallow glass-baking pan. Drizzle fillets with olive oil and lemon juice. Sprinkle with salt, lemon-pepper seasoning and bread crumbs. Drizzle with melted butter and bake 25 to 30 minutes.

Michele's Husband Proof Beef Stroganoff

Bon Appetite!

- 2 lbs. Beef stew meat
- ½ cup flour
- 1 medium onion, chopped
- 2 tablespoons all-purpose seasoning
- 1 tablespoon garlic salt
- ½ stick butter
- 1 cup sour cream
- ½ cup evaporated milk
- ¼ cup water
- 1 (10 ¾ ounce) can cream of mushroom soup
- 1 (10 ¾ ounce) can french onion soup

Melt butter in a medium skillet and season stew beef with all-purpose seasoning. Brown stew meat along with the onions. Add mushroom soup and french onion soup, flour, water and milk. Stir and simmer for 1 to 1 ½ hours. Do not let mixture boil. Add sour cream and heat thoroughly. Serve over cooked noodles.

Tip: Adjust your seasonings by tasting sauce.

Meatloaf with Glaze

- 2 ½ lbs. Ground beef
- 2 eggs, beaten
- I onion, chopped
- I cup breadcrumbs
- 2 packets meatloaf seasoning
- ½ cup cheddar cheese
- ¼ cup milk
- Dash of salt and pepper

In a large bowl combine eggs, meatloaf seasoning, milk and mix. Add remaining ingredients except ground beef. Using your hands add ground beef and mix thoroughly.

Spread into 2 meatloaf pans. Spread glaze onto and bake at 350 degrees 1 hour. Let cool for 15 minutes and remove from pans and place on platter.

Glaze

- I cup light brown sugar
- ½ cup ketchup
- I tablespoon mustard

Mix together brown sugar, ketchup and mustard to make a smooth glaze and spread over meatloaf prior to baking. Adjust ketchup and mustard to get a smooth glaze.

Salmon Croquettes

- 1 (14.75 oz) can Salmon, drained, skin and bones discarded
- ½ cup of buttermilk
- 6 Crackers
- 2 tablespoons of Worcestershire Sauce
- 1 large egg lightly beaten
- 1 Onion, finely chopped
- Season salt and ground black pepper
- Cornmeal for coating

Mix together all ingredients and roll in cornmeal to coat. Shape into hamburger style burgers. Heat skillet. Fry for 3 minutes on eat side and drain on paper towels.

African Chicken and Hot Greens

- 4 or 5 skinless chicken breasts or thighs
- 2 tablespoons salt
- I tablespoon black pepper
- 5 tablespoons olive oil
- 4 medium onions, sliced
- 2 lbs. Kale
- I ½ tablespoons red pepper flakes
- 4 cubes of chicken bouillon
- I-quart water

Wash and pat dry chicken. Season chicken and in a large pot brown chicken in olive oil. Remove chicken and drain oil. Place a layer of onions on the bottom of pan. Top with chicken and a layer of onions and kale. In a separate saucepan, heat water, red pepper flakes and cubes of bouillon and until they have melted. Pour over chicken and kale. Cover and simmer for 2 hours. Do not stir. Serves 6 to 8.

Tip: *This dish is spicy. I love to make a pan of cornbread to go with this dish. I place a piece of cornbread in a bowl and ladle the chicken and greens over it. Delicious!*

Balsamic Chicken

- 1 ¾ lbs. Boneless skinless chicken breast
- 4 oz. Baby portabella mushrooms
- 1 cup onions, diced
- 1 cup baby carrots
- 1 cup green bell pepper
- 2 tablespoons all-purpose seasoning
- 2 tablespoons steak seasoning
- 2 tablespoons balsamic vinegar
- 3 tablespoons olive oil

Cut chicken into 1 ½ inch wide strips and season with all-purpose seasoning and steak seasoning. In large skillet heat olive oil and sauté chicken until brown and thoroughly cooked. Add mushrooms, bell pepper, onions and carrots. Cover and cook for 5 minutes stirring once until vegetables begin to brown. Remove lid and cook 3 more minutes until vegetables are brown. Stir in balsamic vinegar and serve.

Tip: Wipe mushrooms with a damp towel to clean. Never run them under water, as they will be soggy. This is a delicious low calorie dish. Remember you can always adjust seasonings to get the right taste for you.

Country Ham

I made this to take to a friend's family reunion and received one of the best compliments ever. A elderly southern woman who was a guest at the reunion came up to me after eating this ham and said" Now this is what a ham is suppose to taste like". What can I say? I am still grinning.

- I Ham (5 to 6 pounds)
- I ½ cups dark brown sugar
- ¼ cup pineapple juice reserve 3 pineapple slices for garnish
- ¼ cup maple syrup
- ½ teaspoon cinnamon
- ½ teaspoon ginger
- ½ teaspoon allspice
- 15 whole cloves

Preheat the oven to 300 degrees

Mix together brown sugar, pineapple juice, maple syrup, cinnamon, ginger, allspice in a saucepan and heat over medium heat. Bring mixture to a boil. Remove from heat and let cool.

Cut away some of the fat from the ham and with a sharp knife score the ham in a diamond pattern cutting ¼ inch deep so that the glaze penetrates into the ham.

Place ham into roasting pan and spread generously with marinade Reserve a ½ cup of marinade to serve with ham. Stud the ham with whole cloves into the center of each diamond. Cover roasting pan and bake ham for 4 hours basting several times with pan drippings. Remove ham from roaster and place on platter. Serves 6 to 8.

Tip: Ham may be cooked the day of serving or the day before.

Beef Pepper Steak

Curtis and Elaine have been married for over 30 years. So one day I asked Curtis how did he know Elaine was the one for him. He said "I was dating two girls at the same time and what really sealed it for me was the day Elaine made me Beef Pepper Steak and besides she had better legs then the other girl".

- 1 ½ lb round steak
- salt and pepper, to taste
- 1 cup flour
- 2 tablespoons butter
- 2 tablespoons garlic, chopped
- One 10 ½ ounce beef broth
- 2 tablespoons cornstarch
- 1 large onion, cut in strips
- 1 large green bell pepper, cut in strips
- ¼ cup water
- ¼ cup soy sauce

Pound round steak and cut into ¼ inch strips. Brown meat in butter and add garlic and beef broth cover and simmer for 30 minutes. Add cut onion and bell pepper to meat and simmer for 5 minutes. Mix cornstarch, water and soy sauce and add to meat. Simmer until sauce thickens. Season to taste with salt and pepper. Serve over rice.

Garlic Shrimp

- ½ cup olive oil
- 6 cloves of garlic, chopped
- 3 lbs. Prawns or extra large shrimp, shelled and tails left on
- Juice of two limes
- 1 pinch dried oregano
- ¼ cup fresh parsley, chopped
- 1 dash of your favorite hot sauce (optional)

In large skillet heat oil over low heat and cook garlic 1 or 2 minutes do not let it burn. Stir frequently. Bring the heat up to medium and add shrimp and cook until they turn pink. 5 minutes. If you prefer extra oil add it along with the shrimp. Add the lime juice, salt, oregano, parsley to the shrimp and stir well. Adjust seasonings and add hot sauce.

Transfer to a heated serving platter and serve immediately, accompanied by crunchy bread to soak up the garlic-flavored oil. This dish goes well with Mango Couscous.

Pan Seared T-Bone Steaks

- 4 T- Bone Steaks
- 4 tablespoons of Worcestershire sauce
- 4 tablespoons of soy sauce
- 2 tablespoon of all-purpose seasoning
- 2 teaspoons freshly ground pepper
- 4 tablespoon of olive oil

Combine Worcestershire sauce, soy sauce, all-purpose seasoning, salt and pepper in a large bowl. Add steaks and coat both sides. Cover and marinate 1 hour at room temperature. Add olive oil to a large cast iron skillet and sear over medium heat until desired doneness.

Caramelized onions

- 2 large onions, chopped
- 3 cloves of garlic, chopped
- 4 tablespoon olive oil
- 4 teaspoon Sugar

Heat oil in a large skillet over medium low heat. Add onions and sprinkle with sugar. Stir often until onions are caramelized or lightly browned. Pour over meat.

Tip: Marinate meat the day of cooking and cook meat just before serving. Steaks can also be cooked on the grill.

Authentic Quiche Lorraine

- ½ lb. Swiss cheese, grated
- 1/3 cup mushroom slices
- ½ cup cream or half & half
- 3 eggs
- ½ cup mayonnaise
- ¼ cup milk
- 1 tablespoon cornstarch
- ½ cup onion
- Dash of salt and pepper
- Dash of nutmeg and cayenne pepper
- 1 (9 inch) deep-dish pie shell

Preheat oven 350 degrees and pre-bake pie shell for 10 to 15 minutes until lightly brown. Mix together mayonnaise, milk, eggs and cornstarch until smooth. Stir in remaining ingredients. Pour into pie shell and bake at 350 degrees for 35 to 40 minutes or until knife blade comes out clean. Serves 4.

Tip: Quiche is very versatile. Add crumpled bacon or sausage to turn it into a breakfast dish or ground beef or ground turkey for a brunch or dinner meal.

Grilled Tuna Steaks with Peach-Mango Salsa

- 4 (4 ounce) tuna steaks
- ¼ cup olive oil
- ½ teaspoon kosher salt
- ½ teaspoon freshly ground black pepper
- ¼ cup fresh lime juice
- I recipe Peach-Mango Salsa

Preheat grill to 350 to 400 degrees. Lightly oil the food grate and place it 4 inches above the heat. Lightly brush steaks with oil and season each steak salt and pepper and lime juice. Grill steaks to desired doneness approximately 4 to 5 minutes per side. Serve with salsa

Peach-Mango Salsa

1 large peach, peeled and diced
1 green onion, chopped
1 mango, peeled and diced
1 large red pepper, diced
2 tablespoons light brown sugar
2 tablespoons lime juice
2 tablespoons chopped cilantro
1 tablespoon rice vinegar
2 tablespoons chopped garlic
1 teaspoon chopped shallot
¼ teaspoon salt

In a large bowl, combine all ingredients. Cover and chill for 1 to 2 hours.

Tip: This salsa is great with chicken and fish

Fried Chicken

- 1 whole cut-up chicken
- 1 lime
- 3 tablespoons seasoning salt
- 2 tablespoons black pepper
- 2 eggs slightly beaten
- 1 cup buttermilk
- 1 cup flour
- 2 cups of Crisco oil

Wash and pat dry chicken. Place chicken pieces in a bowl and squeeze lime juice over it. Place beaten egg in a small bowl. Place buttermilk into another small bowl and put flour into a medium bowl. Season chicken with seasoning salt and black pepper and dredge into the beaten egg then into buttermilk and finally into the flour. Make sure chicken is covered completely in flour. In a large pot, heat oil. Fry chicken on medium heat for 30 minutes or until done. Remove from heat and drain on paper towels. Serve hot or cold.

Tip: To check and see if oil is hot enough before placing chicken in pan, take a pinch of flour and toss it in the oil. If it sizzles then the oil is ready for the chicken. Again, remember to adjust the seasonings by adding more seasoning salt and pepper.

Corn Beef Dinner

Well, my husband and I have been married for 26 years. I met him in High School; actually I won him on a bet! My girlfriends bet me that I wouldn't be able to get him to notice me. So, I invited him to one of my other friend's parties. Most of the night he ignored me and only said Hi. My curfew was 11:30 p.m. Finally he asked one of my friends to dance and she said "go ask Yvette". We danced two songs and I told him I had to go and gave him a little peck on the cheek. He then planted one back on me! I knew it was love! On my way back home I was driving on the wrong side of the road. We were married about 11 months later and my first meal I made him was beautiful breakfast pancakes, but raw inside... So then I tried Fried chicken for lunch, beautiful brown and crispy on the outside but raw inside.... Well, my wonderful man stuck through it and today I make wonderful pancakes and my chicken is awesome. 26 years later still GOING STRONG!

- 1 (3 to 4 lbs.) corned beef brisket
- ½ cup of chopped onion
- 2 gloves of garlic
- 2 bay leaves
- 6 medium potatoes, peeled
- 6 small carrots
- 6 cabbage wedges
- 1 teaspoon Prepared mustard
- 1 tablespoon brown sugar
- Dash of ground cloves

Place meat in Dutch oven or crock-pot and cover with about 7 cups of water. Add onion, garlic and bay leave. Cover and slow cook 3 to 4 hours or until tender. Remove meat. Add potatoes and carrots to cooking liquid. Cover and bring to a boil for 5 minutes. Add cabbage and cook for 20 minutes or until vegetables are tender. Reserve some of the liquid. Place meat fat side up in a shallow pan and spread with mustard and sprinkle with brown sugar and cloves. Bake in 350-degree oven for 15 minutes. Serve meat with vegetables and reserved liquid. Makes 5 or 6 servings.

Polynesian Chicken

- 4 pounds boneless skinless chicken breasts cut in strips
- ½ cup low-sodium soy sauce
- ½ cup honey
- I can crushed pineapple
- I tablespoon of hoisin sauce
- 2 tablespoon peeled and grated ginger
- 5 green onions sliced
- 1/2 cup chopped fresh cilantro leaves

Preheat oven to 375 degrees. In a large baking pan place the chicken strips. In a medium mixing bowl add honey, soy sauce, hoisin sauce, crushed pineapple and ginger. Stir and pour marinade over entire chicken. Bake for 35-40 minutes.

Sprinkle green onions and cilantro over the top and serve. Serves 6.

Smothered Pork Chops

I wanted to name this recipe" I got you now, Smothered Pork Chops" but I thought it might be a little too much. LOL. I love serving this recipe over white rice.

- 6 thick slices bacon
- I large onion, sliced
- 6 pork chops
- Season salt and pepper, to taste
- I cup all-purpose flour
- 2 tablespoons vegetable oil
- I cup hot water
- I cup milk

Fry bacon in a large skillet on medium heat and remove and drain on paper towels. Saute onion in the same skillet with bacon fat and remove and drain on paper towels. Season pork chops and dredge in flour. Fry on medium heat in same skillet with bacon fat until brown. Remove to a plate. Put remaining flour into skillet, add more oil if necessary, brown flour lightly. Add hot water and then milk. Stir vigorously. Season if desired with more season salt and pepper. Put pork chops, bacon and onions into gravy and reduce heat to simmer. Cover skillet and simmer for 20 minutes. Gravy will thicken on its own. Adjust seasonings.

Beef Tenderloin with Caramelized Onions

- 1 Whole beef tenderloin
- 3 tablespoon olive oil
- 3 tablespoon Soy sauce
- 3 tablespoon Honey mustard
- 3 garlic cloves, minced
- 2 tablespoon Worcestershire sauce
- 1 tablespoon Salt
- 1 teaspoon Black pepper
- 3 tablespoon Italian flavored bread crumbs.

Ask your butcher to prepare the tenderloin by removing the silver lining.

Place tenderloin into a large bowl. Sprinkle with olive oil, soy sauce, Worcestershire sauce, cloves, mustard, salt and pepper. Cover and refrigerate several hours. Place meat in a roasting pan and sprinkle with breadcrumbs.

Preheat oven to 350 degrees. Place tenderloin in roasting pan, cover and bake 1 ½ to 2 hours or to desired doneness. Arrange caramelized onions onto of meat and serve. Serve hot. Serves 6.

Caramelized onions

- 2 large onions, sliced
- 4 tablespoon olive oil
- 4 teaspoon Sugar

Heat oil in a large skillet over medium low heat. Add onions and sprinkle with sugar. Stir often until onions are caramelized or lightly browned. Pour over meat.

Vegetable Kabobs

- 2 red peppers
- 3 yellow potatoes
- 2 green peppers
- 2 zucchini
- 2 red onions
- 12 medium sized mushrooms
- 12 cherry tomatoes

Marinade

- 6 tablespoon Balsamic Vinegar
- 8 tablespoon Extra virgin olive oil
- ½ cup chopped parsley
- 2 teaspoon Salt
- ½ teaspoon Pepper
- 2 tablespoon Lime juice
- 1 tablespoon Sugar

If using wooden skewers soak for 1 hour in cold water. Prepare marinade by placing all the marinade ingredients in a blender and puree. Prepare vegetables by cutting peppers, potatoes, zucchini and onions into ½ inch thick pieces. Leave mushrooms and tomatoes whole. Place skewers through center of the vegetables alternating the pieces. Place skewers on a large baking sheet and coat vegetables with the marinade. Marinade 1 hour before baking or grilling.

Grill or bake in an oven at 375 degrees for 20 to 30 minutes. Serves 5 to 6.

Tip: Marinade can be made in advance and stored in the refrigerator. Vegetables should be prepared the day of serving. You can turn this dish into Shrimp Kabobs by adding shrimp.

Bob's Pulled Pork

- 9 to 10lb Picnic Pork Shoulder Roast (Smithfield at Wal-Mart) bone in
- Hefty EZ Foil Pan (for up to 25lbs)
- 3 Bottles of Kraft-Spicy Honey Barbecue Sauce 18 oz.
- Brown Sugar
- Barbeque Seasoning (Dry)

The fun part is preparing the pork roast for the feast! To begin give the pork shoulder a good rinse in cold water. Gently use a paper towel to the dry the roast. Place the roast in the foil pan. Make sure the fat side is down.

Sprinkle the roast liberally with brown sugar and rub on the top and sides of the roast. For a second time, sprinkle the brown sugar liberally on the roast. Do not rub any further. Sprinkle the roast with the barbeque seasoning. Do not rub.

Add water to the side of the roast until have at least half inch water on the bottom of the pan. The last step before it goes in the oven is to place the aluminum foil. You will need two generous sheets long enough to cover and crimp to the sides of the pan and provide a good seal.

Place the pan on a cookie sheet for added strength. Preheat oven to 350 degrees. Place the pan in the middle of the oven for 7 hours.

After 7 hours in oven remove the roaster and do not peek. Take the pork roast out of the oven and let it rest for 3 hours, it will still be warm. Begin pulling it apart with 2 folks. Fold in the Barbeque sauce. Place pulled pork in crock-pot to warm for 2 hours

Traditional Turkey and Dressing

- I Turkey fresh or frozen, if frozen thaw turkey in the refrigerator 2 days prior to roasting
- Roasting pan
- 3 tablespoons olive oil (flavored oils are fine)
- I orange, quartered
- I onion, quartered
- Butcher's string
- 2 tablespoons seasoning salt
- Salt and pepper to taste

Remove gizzard bag from cavity of turkey. In a medium saucepan season and boil gizzards and contents of bag in water until tender about 2 hours. Add more water during boiling if water gets low. Set aside. Rinse inside and outside of turkey. Pat dry. Pour olive oil over entire turkey, spread evenly. Sprinkle turkey including cavity with seasoning salt, salt and pepper. Place orange and onion quarters into cavity of turkey and tie legs with butcher's string. Tuck wings behind breast. Cover entire turkey and roasting pan with foil. *See Meat Roasting Guide for cooking turkey*

Cornbread Dressing

- 2 boxes Jiffy cornbread mix
- I cup bread crumbs
- contents of gizzard bag, cooked and finely chopped
- I cup onions, finely chopped
- I cup celery, finely chopped
- I medium bell pepper, finely chopped
- 2 tablespoons olive oil
- ½ stick butter
- I ¾ cups of chicken broth
- I small can of mushroom soup
- I tablespoon sage (adjust to taste)
- I tablespoon poultry season (adjust to taste)

Cook cornbread according to directions. Once cooked, crumble and set aside. In a medium skillet, melt butter and olive oil. Sauté onion, bell pepper and celery. In a large mixing bowl add crumbled cornbread, breadcrumbs, chicken broth, mushroom soup, onions, bell pepper, celery and seasonings. Mix well and adjust seasonings if needed. Spread mixture in a medium baking pan and bake on 350 degrees for 25 to 30 minutes. Serves 8-10.

Vegetables

Sweet Potato Souffle

Baked Beans

- 4 slices bacon
- I cup brown sugar
- I onion, chopped
- 3 cans pork and beans
- ¾ cup molasses
- ½ cup barbeque sauce
- I ½ tablespoon yellow mustard
- I ½ tablespoon liquid smoke
- ½ cup ketchup

Fry bacon and crumble. Mix all ingredients together. Pour in a 2 quart glass-baking dish. Bake at 350 degrees for 60 to70 minutes. Remove from oven and let rest for 15 minutes before serving.

Tip: Place a cookie sheet under baking dish when baking, as the dish will bubble. The cookie sheet will catch any spills and save you from cleaning out the oven.

Corn Casserole

- 1 pkg. Jiffy corn muffin mix
- 1 (8 oz). Sour cream
- 1 stick of butter, soften
- 2 eggs
- 1 can cream style corn
- 1 can whole kernel corn. Drained
- ¼ cup sugar

Combine all ingredients and pour into a 1 ½ quart baking dish. Bake at 350 degrees for 45 minutes.

Tips: I like to serve this warm and not hot out the oven. The flavors will be more blended and the taste is yummy. This is a great dish for potlucks!

Mango Couscous

- I cup couscous
- 2 tablespoon olive oil, divided
- I garlic clove, minced
- I mango peeled, pitted and cut into cubes
- (about I cup)
- I jalapeno pepper, seeds and ribs removed, finely chopped
- ½ cup raisins
- I tomato chopped
- I lime juice
- ¼ cup cilantro, chopped
- ¼ cup parsley, chopped
- Kosher Salt

Prepare couscous according to package directions and set aside. In a large pan, heat 1 tablespoon of olive oil on high heat and add mango, garlic and jalapeno pepper until mango is light brown. Add remaining olive oil, raisins, tomato, lime juice, cilantro and heat for 1 minute. Remove from heat and stir in salt to taste. Serves 4.

Tip: *Make sure you assembly all ingredient prior to cooking since you cook this dish on high heat. If you find the heat too hot turn it down a bit. This dish is colorful and great with just about every type of meat especially chicken and pork.*

Aunt Dorothy's Fried Cabbage

- 1 head cabbage, shredded
- 4 slices bacon
- ¼ cup olive oil
- ½ stick butter
- salt and pepper to taste
- 1 medium onion, chopped

In a large skillet fry bacon crisp and remove from pan and drain on paper towel and crumble. Add olive oil and butter to pan along with bacon drippings and slowly melt butter. Turn up heat and add onion and shredded cabbage and stir frequently on medium-high heat until cabbage is tender and golden brown. Add more butter if necessary to skillet.

Green Bean Casserole

- 2 cans french style green beans
- 1 small can sliced mushrooms
- 1 medium onion, chopped
- 1 can cream of mushroom soup
- 1 can French fried onion rings

Combine all ingredients except French fried onions. Put in casserole dish top with onion rings and bake for 30 minutes at 350 degrees.

Honey Glazed Brandied Carrots

- I bag baby carrots
- I cup water
- 3 tablespoons butter
- 3 tablespoons honey
- 2 tablespoons brandy
- 3 tablespoons brown sugar
- Pinch of salt
- I tablespoon chopped parsley

Cook carrots in salted water until they are tender; drain. Place carrots and remaining ingredients in a medium saucepan and simmer over medium heat until carrots are glazed and glossy about 8 to 10 minutes. Serves 6.

Macaroni and Cheese

- 2 cups of corkscrew or elbow noodles
- ½ stick tablespoons butter
- 2 tablespoons all-purpose flour
- 1 cup milk
- 1 cup half & half
- 2 cup Velveeta cheese, cubed
- ½ cup shredded cheddar cheese
- Salt and pepper to taste

Cook noodles according to package directions. Drain and set aside. Preheat oven to 350 degrees. In a large saucepan melt butter. Stir in flour and cook 1 minute. On medium heat add milk and half and half and cook stirring frequently for 5 minutes until slightly thickened and bubbly. Reduce heat to low and add cheeses until melted. Stir in noodles and salt and pepper to taste. Transfer to 3-quart baking dish and sprinkle with cheddar cheese. Bake 20 to 30 minutes until top is lightly brown. Let set 15 minutes prior to serving. Serves 8 to 10.

Oven Roasted Vegetables

- 2 red potatoes
- I sweet potato, peeled
- I red bell pepper
- I green bell pepper
- I box small cremini mushrooms
- Olive oil
- Kosher salt and pepper

Rough chopped all ingredients except mushroom. Place all in a baking dish along with mushrooms and drizzle with olive oil and kosher salt and pepper. Mix well to coat all the vegetables. Bake at 400 degrees for 45 to 55 minutes.

Tip: This is a hearty dish that can be made with any "hardy" vegetables. Do not use soft veggies such as tomatoes. Remember do not run mushrooms under water to clean. Use a damp soft towel and wipe each one separately to clean.

Whipped Mashed Potatoes

We had been dating for about 4 months when my [now] husband accompanied me to our first family function together, a cousin's wedding. The menu had Jamaican food as well as American food. When my father returned to the table from the buffet, he said to my [now] husband, "this curry goat is so good, don't you want to try it? My husband respectfully replied "no thank you sir, I'm a Capricorn, that would be cannibalism!"

Needless to say, when we were married in Negril a few years late. Goat was not on the menu. We still tease him about it to this day.

- 6 red potatoes, peeled
- Salt and pepper to taste
- ½ cup milk
- ¾ stick butter

Quarter potatoes for faster cooking and place in pan and boil until soft. Drain and place in mixing bowl. While potatoes are still hot add butter, milk and salt and pepper and use a hand mixer to beat ingredients together until smooth. Adjust butter, seasonings and milk to your taste and to get the right consistency. Potatoes should be thick and not too soft.

Tip: *You can use a potato masher instead of whipping the potatoes. Use a folk to test doneness of potatoes. Use real butter on the potatoes it really does make a difference. The potatoes taste so much better.*

Steamed Rice

It took me years to figure out how to make a good pot of rice. Finally, one day after I got the water boiling and put in the rice, the phone rang and I turned down the heat to low and covered the pan. When I remembered it about 45 minutes later it was perfect.

- 4 cups water
- 2 cups uncooked rice
- Dash of salt

Bring water to a boil in a medium saucepan. Add salt and rice. Stir once to combine rice with water and return water to a boil. Cover and turn down heat to low and let cook 45 to 50 minutes. Remove saucepan from heat and fluff with fork and serve hot.

Sweet Potato Bake

- 3 cups peeled, mashed sweet potatoes or yams
- I cup sugar
- 2 eggs
- 1/3 cup butter, melted
- I teaspoon of cinnamon
- I teaspoon of vanilla
- ¼ teaspoon ground nutmeg
- ¼ cup of heavy cream, whole milk or half and half

Preheat oven to 325 degrees. Mix all ingredients together except cream with a hand mixer until smooth. Add cream and mix well. Pour into greased casserole dish. Add topping and bake 25 to 30 minutes.

Topping

- I cup brown sugar
- 1/3 cup all-purpose flour
- I cup chopped walnuts
- 4 tablespoons butter, melted

Using folk mix together and sprinkle on top of casserole.

Vegetable Rice

- 2 cups rice
- 2 tablespoons olive oil
- I large onion, chopped
- I garlic clove, chopped
- I green bell pepper, seeded and chopped
- I yellow bell pepper, seeded and chopped
- 2 ripe tomatoes, seeded and chopped
- 1 ½ tablespoons of salt
- ¼ tablespoon black pepper
- 3 chicken bouillon cubes
- I small package frozen green peas
- 4 cups boiling water

Preheat oven to 350 degrees. Add all ingredients to boiling water and return to a boil. Transfer to a 2 quart baking dish and bake for 30 to 40 minutes. Serve 6 to 8.

Stuffed Shell Squash

- 1 (26 ounce) jar pasta sauce
- 24 jumbo shells
- 12 ounces of cooked squash or frozen
- 3/4 cup ricotta cheese
- 1/3 cup grated Parmesan cheese
- 1 egg, slightly beaten
- 2 tablespoons chives
- 2 tablespoons dry bread crumbs
- 1 teaspoon freshly ground nutmeg
- Mozzarella cheese

Preheat oven to 350. Coat a 13x9" baking dish with cooking spray. Spread half the pasta sauce over the bottom of baking dish. Prepare shells according to package directions. Drain. Spread evenly over the pasta sauce.

Meanwhile in a medium bowl, combine the squash, ricotta, Parmesan cheese, egg, breadcrumbs, chives and nutmeg. Mix. Evenly spread the squash mixture over the shells. Arrange in a single layer in the prepared baking dish. Pour remaining sauce over the filled shells and squash mixture. Top with desired mozzarella cheese.

Cover with foil and bake 20 minutes. Remove foil and bake for 5 minutes until bubbly. Serves 8.

Steamed Asparagus Spears

- One bunch of Asparagus spears
- 2 tablespoon butter
- ½ teaspoon salt
- 3 cups water

Place water in the bottom half of steamer pan. Add salt and butter and bring to a boil. Trim the dry ends off the asparagus. If asparagus is thick, peel them lightly. Put asparagus in the top half of the steamer pan and steam for 5 to 10 minutes until tender.

Tip: If you do not have a steamer pan, use a steamer basket inserted in a large pot.

Black-eyed Peas Wrap

- 1 can of black-eyed peas, drained
- 1 tablespoon olive oil
- ¼ cup onions, chopped
- 1 can of Rotel green chilies, undrained
- 1 small can of diced tomatoes, drained
- 2 tablespoons of cilantro or parsley, chopped
- 1 teaspoon cumin
- 2 garlic cloves, chopped
- 2 tablespoons fresh lime juice
- Salt and pepper to taste
- 4 flour tortillas
- Cheese and sour cream (optional)

Heat olive oil in skillet and sauté onions until tender. Mix in black-eyed peas, green chilies, diced tomatoes, cilantro or parsley, cumin, garlic, lime juice and season with salt and pepper to taste. Cook until heated. Spoon mixture onto warm tortillas. Roll and serve. Top with cheese and sour cream, if desired.

Desserts

Strawberry Champagne
Shortcake

Strawberry Tarts

- 5 containers of strawberry yogurt
- 1 ½ cups cool whip
- 2 packages of keebler tart cups
- Fresh strawberry slices for garnish

In a medium bowl combine yogurt and cool whip. Mix well. Slice strawberries and add one slice to each tart cup. Fill tart cup with yogurt and cool whip mixture and add garnish each tart with strawberry slices. Refrigerate and chill for 2 hours prior to serving. Makes 12 individual tarts.

Tip: *Tarts can be made the day prior to serving and placed in the refrigerator on a cookie sheet covered with saran wrap.*

Banana Royal Bake

- 6 bananas- sliced lengthwise
- ½ cup light brown sugar
- ½ cup raisins
- ½ cup unsalted butter
- ½ cup pecans, chopped
- I tablespoon brandy

Line bottom of heavily buttered 9x13 inch baking pan with half of the bananas. Sprinkle with brown sugar and dot with butter.

Spinkle half the raisins and pecans. Repeat layers until all ingredients are used. Bake at 350 degrees for 30 minutes. Cool for 5 minutes and sprinkle with brandy and serve with vanilla ice cream.

Gwen's No Bake Cookies

- 2 cup sugar
- ½ cup cocoa
- ½ cup milk
- ½ cup peanut butter
- ½ cup butter
- 1 teaspoon vanilla
- 3 cups quick oats

Mix sugar, cocoa, milk, peanut butter and butter in a medium saucepan. Bring to a full boil, boil for 1 minute, stirring constantly. Remove saucepan from heat and stir in oaks and vanilla. Drop by spoonfuls onto wax paper and let cool until hardened.

Butterscotch Oatmeal Cookies

- 2 sticks butter, softened
- I cup firmly packed light brown sugar
- ½ cup sugar
- 2 eggs
- I teaspoon vanilla
- I ½ cup all-purpose flour
- I teaspoon baking soda
- I teaspoon cinnamon
- ½ teaspoon salt
- I ½ cup butterscotch chips

Preheat oven to 350 degrees. Beat together butter, and sugars until creamy. Add eggs and vanilla beat well. Add flour, baking soda, salt and cinnamon. Mix well. Stir in oaks. Add butterscotch chips last. Mix well and drop by rounded tablespoons onto ungreased cookie sheet. Bake 10-12 minutes or until golden brown. Cool. Makes 3-4 dozen.

Easy No-Bake Cheese Cake

I was with a pal on his motorcycle, when we pulled up to one of his friend's home. There she was, in there, slicing, dicing and chopping. I was outside, staring at her. Just drinking a beer. The way she used what little she had to cook was amazing to me. So simple, so sweet, I stood and watched her clean the chicken, chop the garlic and onions. Her family was all around, waiting, for she was the family cook. Eventually, she finished and brought out plates and bowls for the little kids full of food. I was standing there, empty handed, starving. She ended up bringing me a whole tray full of food, with a side salad; curry chicken, fried dumplings and other vegetables. She knew I loved beer and she kept them coming! My stomach looked like I was 6 months pregnant when I finished eating.

I ended up marrying that woman.

- 1 8 oz. Package cream cheese, softened
- 1 can condensed milk
- ½ cup lemon juice
- 1 teaspoon vanilla
- 1 9 inch graham cracker crust
- 1 can cherry pie filling

Beat cream cheese until smooth. Gradually add in condensed milk, beat until smooth. Stir in lemon juice and vanilla. Spread in graham cracker crust and refrigerate until firm. Top with chilled cherry pie filling.

Chocolate Chip Cookie Bars

- 2 ¼ cup flour
- I teaspoon baking soda
- I teaspoon salt
- 2 sticks butter, soften
- ¾ cup sugar
- ¾ cup brown sugar
- I teaspoon vanilla
- 2 large eggs
- I ¾ cup chocolate chips

Preheat oven to 375 degree. Combine flour, baking soda and salt in a medium-mixing bowl. In another medium bowl beat butter, sugar and vanilla. Add eggs and beat well. Gradually add flour mixture to butter mixture. Stir in chocolate chips. In a 8x11 greased baking pan spread evenly. Bake 20 to 25 minutes until golden brown. Makes 3 dozen bars.

Sweet Potato Pie

- 2 sticks butter, softened
- 2 cups cooked, peeled mashed sweet potatoes
- 1 ½ cups of sugar
- ½ cup plus 2 tablespoons of evaporated milk
- 1 teaspoon vanilla extract
- 2 eggs, beaten
- 1 ½ teaspoon ground cinnamon
- 1 ½ teaspoon ground allspice
- 2 prepared pie shells, unbaked

Mix butter, potatoes, sugar and evaporated milk until well blended. Add vanilla, eggs, cinnamon and allspice. Mix well. Bake at 350 degrees for about 1 hour and 15 minutes. Serve warm or cold with whipped topping if desired.

Strawberry Champagne Shortcake

- 2 cups all purpose flour
- ½ cup sugar
- I tablespoon baking powder
- ½ teaspoon baking soda
- ½ teaspoon ground cinnamon
- ½ teaspoon salt
- ½ cup unsalted butter, softened
- ¼ teaspoon champagne extract
- ¼ cup strawberry puree
- ¼ cup heavy cream
- Whipped topping

Preheat oven to 400 degrees. In a medium mixing bowl combine flour, sugar, baking powder, baking soda, cinnamon, salt and ¼ cup butter. Stir in champagne extract, strawberry puree and cream. Using a ¼ measuring cup drop on baking sheet. Brush with remaining butter and sprinkle lightly with sugar and cinnamon. Bake 15 to 20 minutes until golden brown. Cool. Makes 12 shortcakes.

Strawberry Puree

- 2 pints strawberries, hulled and halved
- ½ cup sugar

In a blender add strawberries and sugar and blend. Use ¼ cup for the recipe and reserve the rest to serve along with the shortcakes. Garnish with strawberry slices and whipped topping

Tip: Champagne extract is sold online or at your local craft store

Quick Fudge

- 1 cup sugar
- 2/3 cup evaporated milk
- 1 tablespoon butter
- ½ teaspoon salt
- 1 six-ounce bag semisweet chocolate chips
- 1 teaspoon vanilla
- 1 cup chopped pecans (optional)
- 16 large marshmallows

In a medium saucepan combine sugar, milk, butter and salt. Bring to a boil and cook for 5 minutes, stirring constantly. Add chocolate chips and continue to heat and stir until chocolate is melted. Remove from heat and stir in marshmallows, vanilla and nuts. Mix well. Pour mixture into shallow 8-inch square pan to cool. Cut into squares. Makes 2 lbs of candy.

Georgia Peach Cobbler

- 4 whole peaches, peeled, pitted and sliced
- 2 deep-dish frozen pie crusts, thaw
- 2 cups of sugar
- 1 teaspoon almond extract
- ¼ teaspoon vanilla extract
- 1 stick butter
- ¼ teaspoon cinnamon
- 1/8 teaspoon nutmeg
- 1/8 teaspoon cloves
- ¼ teaspoon allspice
- 2 tablespoon cornstarch

Use one of the piecrust, sprinkle lightly with some sugar and cinnamon and drizzle with ¼ tablespoon melted butter. Bake at 325 degrees for 5 minutes. Remove from oven. In a large saucepan combine peaches, sugar, almond and cinnamon extract, nutmeg, cloves, allspice and cornstarch. Bring to a boil, stir to mix thoroughly and remove from heat and pour in baked piecrust. Slice remaining butter and dot pie. Take other piecrust from shell and place on top of peach mixture covering the entire pie and pinch the edges close. Using a knife cut 2 or 3 slits on top of pie to let air escape. Bake at 325 degrees for 40 minutes or until golden brown and bubbly.

Tip: *Place a cookie sheet under the pie when baking to catch any overflow. You can use Apples instead of peaches.*

Chocolate Covered Strawberries

- I pound fresh strawberries with leaves
- 16 ounces milk chocolate chips
- 2 tablespoons shortening
- Toothpicks
- Wax paper

Insert a toothpick in the tops of the strawberries. In a double boiler, melt chocolate and shortening stirring until smooth. Holding the strawberry by the toothpick, dip into the chocolate mixture. Place dipped strawberry on a sheet of wax paper and repeat with the next strawberry.

Tip: Chocolate can be tricky. So here is a tip to keep your chocolate from becoming too thick. When you are melting the chocolate in a double boiler, do not let the water touch the bottom of your upper pan. Heat until only half the chocolate is melted then removed from heat and stir gently until the rest is melted. The chocolate will be cool or tepid to touch. If it's hot, it will become thicken, and no amount of heating or stirring will fix it.

Baked Apples with Caramel Sauce

- 6 Granny Smith apples
- ½ teaspoon nutmeg
- I teaspoon cinnamon
- ½ cup sugar
- I cup apple juice
- 2 tablespoons butter

Preheat oven to 325 degrees. Core apples, do not puncture bottom of apples. Skin ½ inch around top of apples. In a mixing bowl combine nutmeg, cinnamon and sugar. Fill each apple cavity with mixture. Top each apple with a dot of butter. Place apples in casserole dish and pour apple juice around them. Bake for 1½ hours. Drizzle with caramel sauce and serve immediately.

Caramel Sauce

- I stick butter
- I cup light brown sugar
- ¼ cup evaporated milk
- ½ teaspoon vanilla

Melt butter, brown sugar and evaporated milk in a saucepan over medium heat. Stir constantly until bubbly. Cook for 2 to 3 minutes. Remove from heat and add vanilla. Drizzle over baked apples. Serves 6.

Coconut Toto

- ¼ cup butter
- I cup sugar
- 2 eggs
- I teaspoon vanilla
- 3 cups all-purpose flour
- 3 teaspoons baking powder
- I teaspoon cinnamon
- I teaspoon nutmeg
- I teaspoon salt
- 2 cups grated coconut
- I cup evaporated milk

Cream butter and sugar. Add eggs and vanilla and beat for 2 minutes. Sift flour, baking powder, salt, cinnamon and nutmeg.

Add flour mixture to butter and sugar, stir in evaporated milk mix well. Spread evenly in a shallow greased baking pan. Bake at 400 degrees for 30 minutes.

A Handy Spice & Herb Guide

ALLSPICE- a pea-sized fruit that grows in Mexico, Jamaica, Central and South America. Its delicate flavor resembles a blend of cloves, cinnamon, and nutmeg. USES: (whole) Pickles, meats, boiled fish, gravies; (ground) Puddings, relishes, fruit preserves, baking.

BASIL- the dried leaves and stems of an herb grown in the United States and North Mediterranean area. Has an aromatic, leafy flavor. USES: For flavoring tomato dishes and tomato paste, turtle soup; also use in cooked peas, squash, snap beans; sprinkle chopped over lamb chops and poultry.

BAY LEAVES- the dried leaves of an evergreen grown in the eastern Mediterranean countries. Has a sweet, herbaceous floral spice note. USES: For pickling, stews, for spicing sauces and soup. Also use with a variety of meats and fish.

CARAWAY- the seed of a plant grown in the Netherlands. Flavor that combines the tastes of anise and dill. USES: For the cordial Kummel, baking breads; often added to sauerkraut, noodles, cheese spreads. Also adds zest to French fried potatoes, liver, canned asparagus.

CURRY POWDER- a ground blend of ginger, turmeric, fenugreek seed, as many as 16 to 20 spices. USES: For all Indian curry recipes such as lamb, chicken, and rice, eggs, vegetables, and curry puffs.

DILL- the small, dark seed of the dill plant grown in India, having a clean, aromatic taste. USES: Dill is a predominant seasoning in pickling recipes; also adds pleasing flavor to sauerkraut, potato salad, cooked macaroni, and green apple pie.

MACE- the dried covering around the nutmeg seed. Its flavor is similar to nutmeg, but with a fragrant, delicate difference. USES: (whole) For pickling, fish, fish sauce, stewed fruit. (Ground) Delicious in backed goods, pastries, and doughnuts, adds unusual flavor to chocolate desserts.

MARJORAM- an herb of the mint family, grown in France and Chile. Has a minty-sweet flavor. USES: In beverages, jellies, and to flavor soups, stews, fish, sauces. Excellent to sprinkle on lamb while roasting.

OREGANO- a plant of the mint family and a species of marjoram of which the dried leaves are used to make an herb seasoning. USES: An excellent flavoring for any tomato dish, especially pizza.

PAPRIKA- a mild, sweet red pepper growing in Spain, Central Europe, and the United States. Slightly aromatic and prized for brilliant red color. USES: A colorful garnish for pale foods, and for seasoning Chicken Paprika, Hungarian Goulash, salad dressings.

POPPY- the seed of a flower grown in Holland. Has a rich fragrance and crunchy, nut-like flavor. USES: Excellent as a topping for breads, rolls, and cookies. Also delicious in buttered noodles.

ROSEMARY- an herb (like a curved pine needle) grown in France, Spain, and Portugal, and having a sweet fresh taste. USES: In lamb dishes, in soups, stews, and to sprinkle on beef before roasting.

SAGE- the leaf of a shrub grown in Greece, Yugoslavia, and Albania. Flavor is camphoraceous and minty. USES: For meat and poultry stuffing, sausages, meat loaf, hamburgers, stews and salads.

THYME- the leaves and stems of a shrub grown in France and Spain. Has a strong, distinctive flavor. USES: For poultry seasoning, croquettes, fricassees, and fish dishes. Also tasty on fresh sliced tomatoes.

TURMERIC- a root of the ginger family, grown in India, Haiti, Jamaica, and Peru, having a mild, ginger-pepper flavor. USES: As a flavoring and coloring in prepared mustard and in combination with mustard as a flavoring for meats, dressings, salads.

Layer Cake
or Pie Pan   Ring Mold

Baking or
Square Pan

Bundt Tube   Brioche Pan   Angel Cake Pan   Loaf Pan

Common Baking Dishes and Pans

Weight & Measure Equivalents

Equivalent Dishes

4-CUP BAKING DISH

= 9" pie plate

= 8" x 1 ¼" layer cake pan

= 7 ⅜" x 3 ⅝" x 2 ¼" loaf pan

6-CUP BAKING DISH

= 8" or 9" x 1 ½" layer cake pan

= 10" pie pan

= 8 ½" x 3 ⅝" x 2 ⅝" loaf pan

8-CUP BAKING DISH

= 8" x 8" x 2" square pan

= 11" x 7" x 1 ½" baking pan

= 9" x 5" x 3" loaf pan

10-CUP BAKING DISH

= 9" x 9" x 9" square pan

= 11 ¾" x 7 ½" x 1 ¾" baking pan

= 15" x 10" x 1" flat jelly roll pan

12-CUP BAKING DISH OR MORE

= 13 ½" x 8 ½" x 2" glass baking dish

= 13" x 9" x 2" metal baking dish

= 14" x 10 ½" x 2 ½" roasting pan

Total Volume of Pans

TUBE PANS

7 ½" x 3" Bundt tube	6 cups
9" x 3 ½" fancy or Bundt pan	9 cups
9" x 3 ½" angel cake pan	12 cups
10" x 3 ¾" Bundt tube	12 cups
9" x 3 ½" fancy tube mold	12 cups
10" x 4" fancy tube mold	16 cups
10" x 4" angel cake pan	18 cups

SPRING FORM PANS

8" x 3" pan	12 cups
9" x 3" pan	16 cups

RING MOLDS

8 ½" x 2 ¼" mold	4 ½ cups
9 ¼" x 2 ¾" mold	8 cups

Weight and Measure Equivalents

Dash or pinch= less than 1/8 teaspoon

1 ½ teaspoons= ½ tablespoon

3 teaspoons= 1 tablespoon; ½ fluid ounce

2 tablespoons= 1/8 cup; 1 fluid ounce

4 tablespoons= ¼ cup; 2 fluid ounces

8 tablespoons= ½ cup; 4 fluid ounces

12 tablespoons= ¾ cup; 6 fluid ounces

16 tablespoons= 1 cup; 8 fluid ounces; ½ pint

1/8 cup= 2 tablespoons; 1 fluid ounce

¼ cup= 4 tablespoons; 2 fluid ounces

1/3 cup= 5-1/3 tablespoons

½ cup= 8 tablespoons; 4 fluid ounces

¾ cup= 12 tablespoons; 6 fluid ounces

1 cup= 16 tablespoons; 8 fluid ounces; ½ pint

2 cups=1 pint; 16 fluid ounces

4 cups=2 pints; 1 quart; 32 ounces

1 quart= 4 cups; 32 fluid ounces

4 quarts= 16 cups; 1 gallon

16 ounces= 1 pound

Emergency Ingredient Substitutions

Buttermilk

1 cup= 1 tablespoon lemon juice or white vinegar plus enough milk to measure 1 cup.

Corn Syrup, light

1 cup= ¾ cup sugar plus ¼ cup water

Corn Syrup, dark

1 cup= ¾ cup light corn syrup plus ¼ cup molasses

Cream, half and half

1 cup= 1 tablespoon melted butter plus milk to measure 1 cup

Egg

1 whole= 2 egg whites or 2 egg yolks

Honey

1 cup= 1 ¼ cups sugar plus ¼ cup water

Lemon Juice

1 teaspoon= 1 teaspoon cider vinegar

Milk, whole

1 cup= ½ cup evaporated milk; 1/3 cup dry milk powder

Sour cream

1 cup= 1 cup plain yogurt

Sugar

1 cup= 1 cup brown sugar

Helpful Cooking Hints

- Frozen gravies or sauces may be a little thicker after thawing than when they were freshly made. Adding a little appropriate liquid – milk, broth, or bouillon – will thin them to the desired consistency.
- Completely read entire recipe prior to preparing
- Assembly all ingredients prior to cooking
- A little sugar will bring out flavors even in vegetables
- For extra juicy, extra nutritious hamburgers, add ¼ cup evaporated milk per pound of meat before shaping.
- To ripen green pears, just place 2 or 3 in a brown bag, loosely close, and store at room temperature out of direct sunlight.
- Lemon gelatin dissolved in 2 cups of hot apricot nectar with 1 tsp. of grated lemon added for zip makes a perfect base for jellied fruit salad.
- Put a tablespoon of butter in the water when cooking rice, dried beans, macaroni, to keep it from boiling over. Always run cold water over it when done to get the starch out. Reheat over hot water, if necessary.
- Never put a cover on anything that is cooked in milk unless you want to spend hours cleaning up the oven when it boils over.
- Anything that grows under the ground, start off in cold water – potatoes, beets, carrots, etc. Anything that grows above ground, start off in boiling water – English peas, greens, beans, etc.
- To clean aluminum pots when they are stained dark, merely boil with a little cream of tartar, vinegar or acid foods.
- Baking powder will remove tea or coffee stains from china pots or cups.
- Hard-boiled eggs will peel easily if cracked and placed in cold water immediately after taking out of the hot water.
- You can cut a pie cleanly by coating both sides of the knife lightly with butter.

- When recipe calls for adding raw eggs to hot mixture, always begin by slowly adding a small amount of the hot mixture to the beaten eggs to avoid curdling.
- To keep icings moist and to prevent cracking, add a pinch of baking soda to the icing.
- If soup tastes very salty, a raw piece of potato placed in the pot will absorb the salt.
- Pour water into mold and then drain before pouring in mixture to be chilled. Will come out of mold easier.
- When rolling cookie dough, sprinkle board with powdered sugar instead of flour. Too much flour makes the dough heavy. When freezing cookies with a frosting, place them in freezer unwrapped for about 2 hours – then wrap without worrying about them sticking together.

Meat Roasting Guide

Cut	Weight (Pounds)	Approx. Time (Hours) 325° oven	Internal Temperature
BEEF	4	1 ¾	140° (rare)
Standing Rib Roast		2	160° (medium)
(10 inch) ribs		2 ½	170° (well done)
*If using shorter cut			
(8 inch) ribs, allow	8	2 ½	140° (rare)
30 min. longer		3	160° (medium)
		4 ½	170° (well done)
Rolled Ribs	4	2	140° (rare)
		2 ½	160° (medium)
		3	170° (well done)
	6	3	140° (rare)
		3 ¼	160° (medium)
		4	170° (well done)
Rolled Rump	5	2 ¼	140° (rare)
(Roast only if high quality.		3	160° (medium)
Otherwise, braise)		3 ¼	170° (well done)
Sirloin tip	3	1 ½	140° (rare)
(Roast only if high quality.		2	160° (medium)
Otherwise, braise)		2 ¼	170° (well done)
	6	3	175° (medium)
LAMB		3 ½	180° (well done)
	8	4	175° (medium)
		4 ½	180° (well done)
VEAL	5	2 ½ to 3	170° (well done)
Leg (piece)	6	3 ½	170° (well done)
Shoulder	3 to 5	3 to 3 ½	170° (well done)
Rolled Shoulder			

Poultry Roasting Guide

Type of Poultry	Ready-To-Cook Weight	Oven Temperature	Approx. Total Roasting Time
TURKEY	6 to 8 lb.	325°	2 ½ to 3 hr.
	8 to 12 lb.	325°	3 to 3 ½ hr.
	12 to 16 lb.	325°	3 ½ to 4 hr.
	16 to 20 lb.	325°	4 to 4 ½ hr.
	20 to 24 lb.	300°	5 to 6 hr.
CHICKEN	2 to 2 ½ lb.	400°	1 to 1 ½ hr.
	2 ½ to 4 lb.	400°	1 ½ to 2 ½ hr.
	4 to 8 lb.	325°	3 to 5 hr.

Microwave Hints

1. Place an open box of hardened brown sugar in the microwave oven with one cup hot water. Microwave at high for 1 ½ to 2 minutes for ½ pound or 2 to 3 minutes for 1 pound.

2. Soften hard ice cream by putting it in the microwave. One pint will take 15 to 30 seconds; one quart, 30-45 seconds; and one-half gallon, 45 seconds to one minute.

3. One stick of butter or margarine will soften in 1 minute when put in the microwave.

4. Soften one 8-oz package of cream cheese in the microwave for 2 to 2 ½ minutes. One 3-oz package of cream cheese will soften in 1 ½ to 2 minutes.

5. Thaw frozen orange juice right in the container. Remove the metal top lid. Place the opened container in the microwave and heat on high power 30 seconds for 6 ounces and 45 seconds for 12 ounces.

6. Thaw whipped topping…a 4 ½ oz carton will thaw in 1 minute on the defrost setting. Whipped topping should be slightly firm in the center but it will blend well when stirred. Do not over thaw!

7. Soften Jell-o that has set up too hard – perhaps you were to chill it until slightly thickened and forgot it. Heat on a low power setting for a very short time.

8. Dissolve gelatin in the microwave. Measure liquid in a measuring cup, Add Jello and heat. There will be less stirring to dissolve the gelatin.

9. Heat hot packs in the microwave. A wet fingertip towel will take about 25 seconds. It depends on the temperature of the water used to wet the towel.

10. To scald milk, cook 1 cup milk for 2-2 ½ minutes, stirring once each minute.

11. To make dry bread crumbs, cut 6 slices of bread into ½-inch

cubes. Microwave in 3-quart casserole for 6-7 minutes, or until dry, stirring after 3 minutes. Crush in blender.

12. Refresh stale potato chips, crackers, or other snacks of such type by putting a plateful in the microwave oven for about 30-45 seconds. Let stand for 1 minute to crisp. Cereals can also be crisped.

13. Nuts will be easier to shell if you place 2 cups of nuts in a 1-quart casserole with 1 cup of water. Cook for 4 to 5 minutes and the nut meats will slip out hole after cracking the shell.

14. When thawing hamburger meat, the outside will many times begin cooking before the meat is completely thawed. Defrost for 3 minutes, then remove the outside portions that have defrosted. Continue defrosting the hamburger, taking off the defrosted outside portions at short intervals.

15. To drain fat from hamburger while it is cooking in the microwave oven (one pound will cook in 5 minutes on high), cook it in a plastic colander placed inside a casserole dish.

16. Cubed meat and chopped vegetables will cook more evenly if cut uniformly.

17. For stamp collectors: Place a few drops of water on stamp to be removed from envelope. Heat microwave for 20 seconds and the stamp will come right off.

18. Treat fresh meat cuts for 15-20 seconds on high in the microwave oven. This cuts down on meat-spoiling types of bacteria.

19. Do not salt foods on the surface as it causes dehydration (meats and vegetables) and toughens the food. Salt the meat after you remove it from the oven unless the recipes calls for using salt in the mixture.

20. Heat leftover custard and use it as frosting for a cake.

Notes

Notes

Sodium

Sodium is a mineral used by the body to maintain a proper balance of water in the blood. Although it is a vital nutrient, the body needs very little sodium to stay healthy. Because it is found naturally in some foods and is added to many other foods, getting too little sodium is usually not a problem. A high sodium diet, on the other hand, can contribute to high blood pressure in some people. Reducing sodium intake in the diet may help prevent or control high blood pressure. It is hard to know who will develop high blood pressure, or who might benefit from eating less sodium. For these reasons, and because most individuals consume much more sodium than needed, it is generally suggested that we reduce sodium intake.

WAYS TO REDUCE DIETARY SODIUM

- Taste food before salting. Salt food only sparingly at the table.
- Choose foods that have little or no sodium added. In general, the more processed the food, the more sodium it contains. For example, processed turkey breast purchased at a deli has considerably more sodium than fresh turkey breast.
- In many recipes, the salt can be cut back or even eliminated without greatly affecting the taste. Experiment with the recipes, using less salt each time and using low sodium substitutes for high sodium ingredients.
- Read labels on food packages. Compare the sodium content to similar items and to the recommended sodium intake for an entire day.
- Limit intake of high sodium foods such as cheeses, processed meats, soups, broths, snack foods, canned vegetables and vegetable juices, pickled vegetables, gravies, sauces, commercial casserole mixes, frozen dinners, and condiments. In many cases, lower sodium alternatives are available.
- When eating in restaurants, ask for foods to be prepared without

added salt and request to have sauces, gravies, dressings, and condiments served on the side.

- Use herbs and spices instead of salt to enhance flavor of foods. Check the label of seasonings to be sure they do not contain sodium. Use onion powder rather than onion salt, garlic powder instead of garlic salt

Index

DESSERT

Baked Apple w/Carmel Sauce
Banana Royal Bake
Butterscotch Oatmeal Cookies
Chocolate Chip Cookie Bars
Chocolate Covered Strawberries
Coconut Toto
Easy No Bake Cheese Cake
Georgia Peach Cobbler
Gwen's No Bake Cookies
Quick Fudge
Strawberry Champagne Shortcake
Strawberry Tart
Sweet Potato Pie

CPSIA information can be obtained at www.ICGtesting.com
Printed in the USA
LVOW012010011211

257446LV00002B/1/P